If you give
a mom a
martini...

If you give a mom a martini...

100 WAYS TO FIND 10 BLISSFUL MINUTES FOR YOURSELF

Julie Klappas and Lyss Stern

Illustrations by Izak Zenou

Clarkson Potter/Publishers
New York

Grateful acknowledgment is made for the right to reproduce the following:
"Hurry" from THE KINGDOM OF ORDINARY TIME by Marie Howe.
Copyright 2008 by Marie Howe.
Used by permission of W. W. Norton & Company, Inc.

Library of Congress Cataloging-in-Publication Data
Klappas, Julie.
If you give a mom a martini / Julie Klappas and Lyss Stern.—1st ed.
p. cm.
1. Mothers—Anecdotes.   I. Stern, Lyss.   II. Title.

HQ759.S693 2009
306.874'3—dc22   2008040144

ISBN 978-0-307-45371-6

Printed in the United States of America

DESIGN BY JENNIFER K. BEAL DAVIS

1   3   5   7   9   10   8   6   4   2

First Edition

To the loves of my life,
John, Kate, and Tucker,
for reminding me that nothing
is worth more than this day.

—JULIE

For Brian, Jackson, and Oliver.
To love you and to be loved
by you are the greatest joys
of my existence.

—LYSS

foreword

The moment I heard the title of this book, I instantly laughed. After all, I think every mom deserves a "time-out" as often as she can get one!

I always knew I wanted to be a mom. And everything I do is out of a desire to be a better one for my kids. That means not just taking care of my family, but also trying to help take care of the world we live in—so that someday our children will be able to share this beautiful world with *their* children.

There is something I have always been sure of, and that is the power of a mother's love! We would move mountains for our kids. But we also get so busy taking care of everyone else that we always put ourselves last on the list. And that's just not OK!

We are all so lucky to be here, living in this beautiful world. And as moms, we are doubly blessed with the greatest gift: our children. In my opinion, whatever moms can do to stay positive and happy for our kids can't be a bad thing! So go ahead, find a quiet place (hide in a closet if you have to!). Open this book to any page. You'll find ideas that will help you laugh, relax, reflect, rejuvenate, or just breathe. Claim the next ten minutes just for *you*. Your kids will thank you—and you'll be a better mom for it!

—Christie Brinkley,
MOTHER OF THREE AND SUPERMODEL

introduction

We'll make this brief. Because chances are, if you're reading this book, you're:

A. A mom
B. Tired
C. Thinking about the twenty-seven other things you should be doing at this red-hot moment. For your kids. Your job. Your husband. Your house. Your hamster. Your . . . well, you get the picture.

When we sat down to write this book, we wanted to start by saying that above all else, we love motherhood. We love the delicious hugs and the messy spills and the princess obsessions and the five hours of sleep and the pillow forts and the putting-on-our-Superman-capes-at-five A.M.–ness of it all.

But somewhere along the way, we started to feel guilty about taking time out for ourselves. If you've ever locked yourself in the bathroom pretending to "go" in order to buy a few precious minutes alone with *Us Weekly*, you know what we mean. And while we're not knocking hiding in the loo, we think you can do better.

So we decided to give moms the inspiration and the tools to put aside ten precious minutes to do something just for her. When we started writing, our male friends laughed. "Ten minutes? Who doesn't have *ten minutes*?" And our mom friends lamented, "Ten whole minutes? I can't *imagine*." (In fact, out of all the women we've approached about this idea, only *one* responded that she didn't ever need a break from her wonderful children. To her we ask, "What drugs are you on?")

As word got out, we realized that we were onto something. Friends of friends began sending us their secret time-out ideas. Moms begged us to reveal our favorites. And we couldn't wait to call each other after we tried them out ourselves.

The modern mother comes in all shapes and sizes. Given the dizzying variety of choices and responsibilities in her life, we believe that there isn't a mom out there who couldn't use a little sanity break from time to time. So if there's anything we'd like to impart to you, dear Mom, it is this: We're all in this together. And every so often, it's good to do a little something for yourself, because a happier mom is a better mom.

So claim your time. And if anyone in your family balks, explain patiently that out of the 1,440 minutes each day, 10 minutes for Mom seems more than fair. If that doesn't work, standing on a chair and shouting, "I gave you life. Now give me ten minutes!" ought to do it.

Have we taken up too much of your time? OK, we'll wrap this up.

This book is a love letter to the modern mom, a reminder that even the most "together" mothers among us need time to reflect, dream, relax, take care of themselves, and find the positive energy required to go back out there and face the music, even if it is "The Wheels on the Bus."

So get to it. One hundred ways to feel sexier, stronger, and more relaxed await you.

A tall order for ten minutes, you say? Well, turn the page.

A note to the reader: This book is meant to make your life easier and more enjoyable, so use it as you choose. The ideas are in no particular order, so feel free to skip around and go where the mood takes you. And if you're inclined to curl up for ten minutes and use the book as a pillow, hey, that's fine too.

Let It Go to Your Head

Do a handstand. It's a surefire way to clear your mind and feel instantly refreshed. If you do this at a particularly chaotic time in your home, you'll find that peace is instantly restored. After all, what can your kids do to Mom when she's standing on her head?

If you're worried about your balance, practice with a wall behind you. Keeping your weight forward over your hands, push off one foot and swing the other leg up toward the wall. Immediately lift the other leg up to join it. Feel the blood rushing to your head, and enjoy the view.

Pick Your Flix

Update your Netflix queue—it's surprisingly relaxing. "Accidentally" delete any movies chosen by your husband that feature Angelina Jolie wearing leather. Intentionally add any movies with George Clooney wearing anything. Use your discretion about moving Disney films up or down the list, depending on whether your kids are being nice to you at the time. And remember to look surprised several days later when three Nora Ephron comedies arrive in the mail.

Sort Your Skivvies

It may not be glam, but go through your undie drawer and throw out all of your old granny panties. It'll feel great. Sure, you used to have fabulous lingerie before the kids were born. But somewhere along the way, did you go from wearing La Perla to La Fruit of la Loom? If so, our criteria for the big panty purge is to get rid of anything that:

1. has an elasticized waistband hitting above your navel.
2. could mortify you should you be rushed unexpectedly to the ER.
3. would be worn by Bridget Jones on one of her fat days.

And in your next free ten minutes? Order new lingerie online!

4

Recline. Regenerate. Repeat.

TOOLS NEEDED:
Suburban shopping mall, iPod

When you're in the mall with your husband and kids, tell them that you're going to the ladies' room. Then slip into Brookstone, sit in one of their giant massage chairs, and listen to the sounds of the ocean on your iPod.

Judge for Yourself

CONTRIBUTOR:
Kelly Ripa
mother of three and actor

KELLY'S TIP

For a great ten-minute break, I love to get in the kitchen and whip up a really complicated recipe from *Mastering the Art of French Cooking*.

Not really.

Actually, my not-so-secret escape is to watch a few minutes of my idol Judge Judy's TV show. She is so honest and quick and smart. You know how in life you just wish that there were people who had all the answers? She does—and she cuts through all the nonsense. Although ten minutes is not long enough for an entire episode, it'll probably get me through one juicy case. That's OK. I'll take what I can get.

Check out the Good, the Bad, and the Fugly

Still wearing maternity pants a year after giving birth? Don't feel so bad. Log onto gofugyourself.com and be reminded that even gorgeous stars have their moments. This blog, devoted to celebrity fashion faux pas and red-carpet catastrophes, is the textbook definition of guilty pleasure. You can also check out *The Fug Awards* book, which hands out honors such as the Sag Award (for most egregious misuse of breasts) and the Tanorexia Award (for the person most addicted to bronzer). Poring over photos of celebrity fashion disasters may not be the most enriching use of your time, but it will make you feel a wee bit better when your child spills juice on your white shirt. Again.

Get Smart

Think fast: Does a wild turkey sleep in a nest or a tree?

What's the difference between a squid and an octopus?

If you get into a taxi and it goes backward, why do you still have to pay?

When you have ten minutes alone, preferably with a martini, Google the answers to all of your child's questions of the day. Chances are you can come up with a clever response (and feel smarter than a fifth-grader) in less than five minutes. Then, spend the next five minutes chuckling to yourself about how much fun this is: the cocktail, the knowledge, the parenting.

Make It Quick(ie)

Turn on the TV and let the kids loose. Lock the bedroom door and get it on—sprint-style—with your spouse. Phew! It's a great workout and a real pick-me-up for both of you.

Make the Best Martini Ever

Mix it. Pour it. Savor it. If necessary, rinse and repeat.

LEMON DROP MARTINI
(OTHERWISE KNOWN AS MOMMY'S LEMONADE)

Granulated sugar

6 parts lemon-flavored vodka

1 part dry vermouth

Cracked ice

Lemon twist, for garnish

Wet the rim of a martini glass, and press into a plate of granulated sugar. Combine the liquid ingredients in a cocktail shaker with cracked ice, and shake well. Strain into the prepared martini glass, and garnish with a lemon twist.

Browse for Bling

TOOLS NEEDED:
High-end jewelry store, nerve

Stroll into Harry Winston or Tiffany & Co. and try on the most expensive diamonds in the place. Tell the sales associate you need something to go with the Galliano you're wearing to the Oscars.

Get a Face-Lift

Since phones and children do not mix (funny how they suddenly can't live without you as soon as an old friend calls . . .), stay connected on Facebook.com. It's a stealth bridge into the lives of your chums, allowing you to "poke" them quietly while the kids are engrossed in play. See what friends are "doing now," take personality quizzes, play Word Twist, and pose questions to the group about important mommy matters (or the latest Britney meltdown). Then, pore over pictures of the adorable munchkins they're sneaking away from so they can chat on Facebook too.

Stitch 'n Bitch

Make a mad dash to the knitting or craft store. There's usually a big table smack in the middle of the place with an empty chair just waiting for you to soak up the yummy colors and crafty ideas.

For ten minutes, you can usually do one (or more) of the following:

- Flip through the latest issue of *Vogue Knitting*.
- Trade book suggestions.
- Eavesdrop on an intense conversation.
- Bemoan school bureaucracy.
- Try on a sample sweater in a color you wouldn't be caught dead in.
- Admire someone's baby blanket.
- Shop the sale yarns.
- Catch up with old knitting friends who are already firmly ensconced in their seats.

Make It a Laughing Matter

This one's no joke: there's a movement out there called "laughter yoga," and people are joining laughter clubs to practice it worldwide. Laughter yoga is all about simple laughter exercises and gentle yoga breathing, which when practiced in a group turns into real laughter. Some believe the playful, empowering exercises help unwind the negative effects of stress and boost the immune system.

Is laughter really the way to calm a mommy tsunami? Well, who knows? But with more than five thousand laughter clubs in more than fifty countries, why not try it? Laughter sessions generally take a few minutes, and some clubs meet daily. Hey, it's good for a laugh.

To find a laughter club near you, log onto www.laughter yoga.org.

Wax Poetic

If you're having one of those days when you can't seem to find the "me" in your Mommy and Me world, try immersing yourself in a great poem. Download a poetry podcast—it will transport you to another place.

Podcasts called "Poem of the Day" are available through iTunes. Subscribe, and a poem is automatically downloaded to your computer daily. Search poetryfoundation.org or sonibyte.com for a podcast about a specific theme. Or check out poets.org, which allows you to search poems by topic or occasion, such as "gardening" or "Mother's Day."

Here is a poem to put you in the mood:

"HURRY" BY MARIE HOWE

We stop at the dry cleaners and the grocery store
and the gas station and the green market and
hurry up honey, I say, hurry hurry,
as she runs along two or three steps behind me
her blue jacket unzipped and her socks rolled down.
Where do I want her to hurry to? To her grave?
To mine? Where one day she might stand all grown?
Today, when all the errands are finally done, I say to her,
Honey I'm sorry I keep saying hurry—
you walk ahead of me. You be the mother.
And hurry up, she says, over her shoulder, looking
back at me, laughing. Hurry up now darling, she says,
hurry, hurry, taking the house keys from my hands.

CONTRIBUTOR: DANA STANGEL-PLOWE, MOTHER OF THREE DAUGHTERS AND POET

Sing out, Sister

CONTRIBUTOR:
Jill Hennessy,
mother of two and actor

JILL'S TIP

I like to set myself up with a great cup of coffee and some Angelica Cookies (but any cookie would do). I find a quiet place alone with my six-string acoustic guitar and sing some of my favorite songs at the top of my lungs. It's a great way to center myself and get back to sanity—at least a certain level of sanity.

Set a Table for Onesie

Order a take-out meal just for you. Intentionally make it something you know your kids won't eat: the spicier or more exotic, the better. Then, eat by yourself before the kids gobble their nuggets. Or if you're in the mood to cook for yourself, try this comforting ten-minute recipe:

BRUSCHETTA PASTA

- 3 ounces dried pasta (rigatoni or your favorite shape)
- 1 large beefsteak tomato, diced
- 2 tablespoons capers, plus 2 tablespoons caper liquid
- 2 tablespoons pitted black olives (oil cured or kalamata), chopped
- 2 tablespoons good olive oil
  Fresh pepper to taste
- 1 handful fresh basil, torn or chopped
- 1 teaspoon good sea salt

Bring a pot of salted water to a boil, and throw in the pasta. Cook it according to the directions on the box.

While the pasta is cooking, put the diced tomato into a medium-size bowl with the capers, caper liquid, olives, olive oil, salt and fresh pepper. Stir.

Drain the cooked pasta, reserving ¼ cup of the cooking liquid. Toss the pasta with the reserved cooking liquid, all of the combined ingredients, the basil, and the salt, and stir until the pasta is evenly covered. If you want, add more olive oil. If you are dieting, don't.

Grab a fork and lean against the counter, or go into your bedroom or the garage or the bathroom, hide, and eat in peace.

CONTRIBUTOR: MARCEY BROWNSTEIN, MOTHER OF ONE AND OWNER OF MARCEY BROWNSTEIN CATERING AND EVENTS

17

Get Your Pregame On

TOOLS NEEDED:
an alarm clock, a sleeping family

Before your kids wake up, before you feed the dog, before you make the school lunches and turn on your BlackBerry, press the snooze button on life and find more time for yourself. Because chances are the only way to get your own time is to take it before anyone notices. So wake up early! Trading sleep for a few minutes of solitary calm is a great way to get centered and ready to face the day ahead.

Be a Doll

Get lost by spending a few minutes on thisisblythe.com. If you don't know her, Blythe is a doll created in the '70s by designer Allison Katzman. She has eyes that change color with the pull of a string attached to the back of her head. Blythe dolls were sold only for one year in the United States, but she is experiencing a newfound popularity thirty years later. It's easy to become obsessed with Blythe! She's been described as looking like Barbie with elephantiasis or like Christina Ricci, among other things. We think she's gorgeous.

Snap, Push, and Pop

TOOLS NEEDED:
A Bedazzler stud-and-rhinestone setter,
items that need embellishment

Take a few minutes and add some sparkle to your life. Try the Bedazzler (mybedazzler.com). If you don't remember this kitschy, cult product from the '70s, it looks like a giant plastic stapler and is used to insert studs, stars, or rhinestones onto fabric. You can Bedazzle almost anything—hats, shirts, belts, scarves, your daughter's jeans. You'll find it oddly rewarding. To quote the late-night TV commercial that sells it: *Don't be dull—BE DAZZLING! It's easy, fun, and fabulous!* Even if you've never threaded a needle, you can Bedazzle like a pro in minutes.

Throw a (Virtual) Punch

TOOLS NEEDED:

Nintendo Wii game system, cute boxing gloves

Put on your boxing gloves, crank up the *Rocky* soundtrack, and step into the ring for ten minutes of Wii Fight Night. The adrenaline pumps. The crowds cheer. You are Muhammad Ali in your mind. Your stress will be gone, and you'll feel alive.

Work It at the Car Wash

TOOLS NEEDED
Twenty bucks, disheveled car, three guys who perform miracles with a Power Vac

Has your once-spotless car become a depository of spilled snacks, ATM receipts, school art projects, and various articles of child-size clothing? If so, repeat these words: Brushless Car King, take me away!

Visit the car wash, order "the works," and experience instant gratification. Because where else can you hand over something utterly gross and, ten minutes later, see it sparkle like new? Although it usually doesn't last long, it's well worth it. Your vehicle will be restored to its former beauty. Your life will feel in order. And you'll be at least thirty-six cents richer in loose change.

Do Some Good

TOOL NEEDED:
A big heart

Ten minutes is the perfect amount of time to give back to a charity you love. It doesn't have to cost a lot of money. You can write a card for a Habitat for Humanity family, collect change for a penny harvest, or clip some box tops. A donation made to Firstbook.org will provide brand-new books to children in need. Or you can make a difference *and* reduce clutter in your home (bonus!) by filling a bag with stuff you don't need and donating it to someone who does. There, didn't that feel good?

Bat-Her Up!

Go into a batting cage, pretend you are A-Rod (or insert favorite baseball player's name here), and hit the balls as if they were your mother-in-law's face.

Tend to Your Kneads

TOOLS NEEDED:
$12, a manicure salon

This one's a no-brainer: Swing by your local manicure salon for a maxed-out-mommy foot massage. There really is no substitute for getting rubbed by a stranger (to whom you owe nothing but a nice tip).

Ah, the warm-water soak . . . the repetitious kneading of the arches . . . the vibrating chair—it all makes you want to just curl up and suck your own thumb. Pure mom balm.

If you can't get to a manicure place, follow these instructions for a great foot soak you can do at home:

Add 4 cups of warm organic whole milk, 2 tablespoons Epsom salts, and 3 drops of organic lemon essential oil to a warm-water footbath. Soak your feet for 10 minutes, and enter mama nirvana.

Tame Your Arch Enemy

TOOLS NEEDED:

Good quality tweezer (it's worth it to invest in a Tweezerman; they really are the best, and you can pick your favorite color), a regular mirror, a small pair of scissors, Paul & Joe Eyebrow Pencil in Number 2, cooling gel, hairspray or styling gel, a tooth brush or an eyebrow brush.

Good news, moms! The eyebrows that make you look your best can be obtained in your own bathroom—no wax necessary!

LET'S GROOM YOUR BROWS!

1. Tweeze your eyebrows until you get the desired shape. Brows should extend from above your inner eye to beyond the edge of your outer eye.

2. Grab only the strays underneath the arch.

3. Be sure you keep standing back from a regular mirror (not a high-magnification mirror) so you can see the overall effect of your tweezing.

4. Trim the very tips if hairs are long.

5. After you tweeze, apply a balm to help calm the skin. Try Gigi After Wax Cooling Gel, Aloe Vera Cooling Gel, or witch hazel.

6. Use an eyebrow brush or a toothbrush to comb hairs in place.

7. Apply a styling gel (hair spray will also work) to keep hairs in place.

8. When the gel dries, you can apply any eyebrow makeup (such as an eye pencil) needed to enhance the brows.

CONTRIBUTOR: SANIA VUCETAJ, MOTHER OF FOUR AND EYEBROW GURU TO THE STARS

Take a Good Look

CONTRIBUTOR:

Samantha Bee

mother of two and senior correspondent for *The Daily Show with Jon Stewart*

SAMANTHA'S TIP

Whenever the stars align and I get a few uninterrupted minutes of blissful "me time," I head for the nearest high-magnification mirror and treat myself to an intense session of personal grooming. Now, you may say, "Please! That's gross! Leave it to the professionals!" But here's the thing: I love it. I miss it. The world looks at the weird whisker that occasionally grows out of the side of my face and also misses it.

There is nothing more delicious to me than ten minutes to myself, quality natural lighting, and the chance to make sure my fingernails are all the same length. I emerge from my chrysalis refreshed, stray gray hairs plucked, face pink and dewy from a quick enzyme mask, cuticles presentable to other humans, and eyes visible from underneath my former unibrow.

NOTE TO HUSBAND: DON'T GET USED TO IT.

Try This When You're Desperate

Point and yell excitedly to your child, "Hey, look over there. It's Elmo!" That should distract him or her for at least a solid minute.

Sing Loudly and with Abandonment

Sing this song by the comedienne Nancy Lombardo to the tune of "Let It Be" by the Beatles:

When I find the noise too much to cope with,

Everyone is calling me.

I hide out in the bathroom. Let me pee. Let me pee.

I'm tired of these questions,

What's for dinner?

Where can my ball be? I hide out in the bathroom,

Let me pee. Let me pee.

Let me pee. Let me pee. Let me pee. Let me pee.

Mommy needs a time-out.

Let me pee. Let me pee.

Oh no, they're pounding on the door.

No clue where the remote can be?

If you clean, you'll find it.

Let me pee. Let me pee.

For just some moments now and then,

I need a little privacy,

To get my thoughts together.

Let me pee. Let me pee. Let me pee. Let me pee.

Mommy needs a time-out.

Let me pee. Let me pee.

For just ten minutes, let's pretend I'm not here.

For just ten minutes, let's pretend I'm not here

Oh no, I flushed the toilet.

Now they'll know that I will soon be free.

I need to stall for more time.

No more pee. No more pee.

Two men calling out my name.

Well, it used to be my fantasy.

Now it's just a nightmare.

Let me be. Let me be.

Let me be. Let me be. Let me be. Let me be.

Mommy needs a time-out. Let me be. Let me be.

Get Lost

TOOLS NEEDED:
Car, GPS device, good music for the ride

Next time you're out, why not make like a Supertramp and take the long way home? Drive through a wealthy neighborhood, and check out the unreal mansions. Or explore a side street you don't know, and people-watch. When it's time to go back to reality, turn on your navigation system and head back.

Polish It Off

CONTRIBUTOR:
Melissa Joan Hart
mother of two and actor

MELISSA'S TIP

I go get my nails done as an escape from the distractions of home. Afterward I feel a little sexier, and even though it's a small part of my body I've improved, whenever I catch a glimpse of my nails I stand a little straighter and feel a little prettier.

Flirt with a Latte Boy

TOOLS NEEDED:
$4, anonymity

Go to a coffee shop to "*buy a cup of coffee.*" But the real reason you're there (wink, wink) is to flirt with the boy who makes your drink.

Flirting with strangers can be the fastest way to mom-nesia, actually making you feel like a sexual being again. Remember that feeling? Neither do we.

Attempt to engage him in conversation. Be coy. Dust off your best flirty moves (hair flip, batting of the eyes). Instead of wrapping your hands around the steaming cup, imagine wrapping your hands around—well really, do we have to draw you a picture?

If barista boy happens to be on his break, it's not a total loss. You can always sink into a comfy chair and drink your damn coffee.

Make a House Call

The purple powder room! The brown shag rug! What were they *thinking*? Is the grass really greener on the other side of the baby gate? Play out your voyeuristic fantasies by going to an open house in your neighborhood, and find out for yourself. It's a terrific way to take a break from your world and see how other people live (without getting arrested for trespassing). Some model-home showings even include snacks and movies on a tricked-out entertainment system. Kick back on the sofa, and spend a few minutes relaxing—it's like taking a time-out in someone else's (spotless) house.

Fall in (Puppy) Love

TOOL NEEDED:
Fido

Whooozagoodboy? Whoozagoodgoodboy? You are. Oh, yes you are. Oh, YES YOU ARE . . .

Looking for devotion, attention, and a big wet kiss? When your kids won't deliver, spend ten minutes alone with your pooch. Studies show that holding, petting, and talking to your pet can actually lower your blood pressure. We recommend it because a dog or a cat can't talk back, hate the outfit you picked out, or reject the meal you've made for it.

Embrace Your OCD

TOOLS NEEDED:
Fresh face, makeup, pencil sharpener, and brush cleaner

Dump out your makeup drawer, and spend ten minutes cleaning and organizing each tube, brush, and tool. Sort them by brand, color, shape, and frequency of use. Try on a forgotten lipstick with a long-lost gloss or a bold eye shadow with a daring liner that you haven't used in ages. Toss old mascaras, concealers, and lipstick shades that you should never have purchased in the first place. Before you know it, you've given yourself a full makeover and you'll feel beautiful—at least until the baby spits up in your hair.

35
★★★★★

THE ULTIMATE

Way to Green Your Routine

CONTRIBUTOR:
Sophie Uliano
mother of one and author of *Gorgeously Green: Eight Simple Steps to an Earth-Friendly Life*

SOPHIE'S TIP

Take ten minutes out of your day to think about the most important thing you can do as a mom to be green. Going green can be overwhelming—ugh—so much to do, and where on earth do I start? Nonleaching bottles, lead-free lunch boxes, organic mattresses, the list is endless!

So sit down somewhere quiet, take out a pad of recycled paper or an old envelope, and write down ten things that you want to change or investigate in the Green Mom Space. We all want to be eco-friendly moms, so what are you most concerned about? Once you have written down your ten areas of concern, get a red pen and put a number beside each one to denote its priority status.

When I did this exercise as a new mom (no one knew about leaching plastics eight years ago!), my top area of concern was pesticide residue. It was unbearable for me to think of any toxic *anything* going into my little angel's system. I decided then and there to make the switch to going green, at least as far as my baby daughter was concerned. As the months went by, I slowly made my way down the list, which was permanently pinned to my office corkboard. After six months, every concern had been fully addressed—so you can see how invaluable that ten minutes was!

Touch up Your Roots

TOOLS NEEDED:
backyard, garden tools

While it can take a lifetime to create a truly beautiful garden, ten minutes in the dirt can do wonders for your outlook. Dig deep. Work the soil. Take out your frustrations on a rosebush, and find comfort in the fact that those "tough love" cuts will yield a bounty of Floribundas down the line. Getting outside and gardening can be the mood-changing equivalent of washing your face with cold water. Why not cut some flowers or branches and bring them inside to enjoy all week? Your perspective will thank you. And so will your favorite vase.

Soap Up

TOOLS NEEDED:
TV, the patience to program your DVR

Tired of your own mama drama? TiVo a soap opera, and watch a few minutes of someone else's troubles. You'll not only feel blessed that you don't have a split personality or a psychopathic evil twin, you'll also be inspired by some great lines you can use in your own life should the appropriate situation arise.

Our favorite lines (as we remember them) from the aptly titled *All My Children*:

"Men are like puppies. Scratch the right spot and they're yours forever."

—MARIAN COLBY

"I'm totally committed to your happiness."
"If you were committed, I'd be happy."

—MARIAN AND LIZA COLBY

"The last innocent words you uttered were ga-ga-goo-goo!"

—MARIAN COLBY TO PALMER CORTLANDT

"You can't hurt me! I'm Erica Kane!"

—ERICA TO A BEAR (THE BEAR RAN AWAY)

Get Off the List

As a mom, life is all about multitasking and interruptions. So here's something you can do in a flash that will be the easiest thing you've accomplished all day.

If you like catalogs but your mailbox is overflowing with them (Pottery Barn? Hello?) log onto catalogchoice.org, and decline the ones you no longer want to receive. In only a few seconds, you can help the environment and simplify your life. Then, pat yourself on the back by ordering a li'l somethin' for yourself online (no catalog required).

Get the Baby to Pull His Weight

Drowning in domestic drudgery? Get some help. Purchase the Baby Mop, a real product (no joke) that attaches to your child, causing him or her to unsuspectingly dust the floors while crawling.

Get a Handle on It

CONTRIBUTOR:

Shoshanna Lonstein Gruss
mother of one and fashion designer

SHOSHANNA'S TIP

My L.L.Bean canvas tote is my bag of fun. In it, I have everything I need to fill a few minutes of free time with things I love to do. It goes wherever I do. In my bag right now?

- Mementos from my daughter's first year of school, and pictures from my brother's wedding, both to be made into albums for friends and family
- Tear sheets from magazines of things I want to buy online
- Raisin biscuits from the Vermont Country Store (a childhood favorite)
- An article from the *New York Times* Science section, still to be read (this drives my husband crazy, as the news is "old" by now, but it doesn't bother me!)
- *People, Allure, Martha Stewart Living, Details* . . .

I recommend keeping a personal "bag of tricks" to everyone. That way, when you're lucky enough to find a few spare minutes, you can just grab the bag and get busy doing something that makes you happy.

Make Room for Daddy

Plan a grown-up playdate with your man. Read restaurant reviews and scour websites for events listings in your town. Book a babysitter. Pick out a great outfit from the back of your closet that makes you feel sexy. (Remember those?) Then, send him a steamy save-the-date e-mail with the details. If you feel even the slightest bit guilty about a night out without the kids, remember, they could probably use a break from you, too.

Throw Yourself a Mom Prom

Have a high-school reunion with yourself by cracking open your yearbook and looking up old classmates online. Classmates.com, Facebook, MySpace, and Google are good places to start. This can be much more relaxing than a real reunion, as it does not require you to look fabulous, make small talk, or wear a name tag. For the full effect, download songs from your glory days while doing so. (Remember that Phil Collins prom theme?)

For ten minutes, see what ex-boyfriends are doing, tell off old rivals in your mind, and flash back to your pre-mommy glory days, when life was simpler and legs were cellulite-free. Then, feel good about yourself and all that you've accomplished, including finally figuring out your hair. And thank God you're not back there anymore.

Dwell on It

TOOLS NEEDED:
Sunday newspaper, active imagination

There's nothing like poring over the Sunday Real Estate section to really fantasize about what you would do with $60 million. Location? Definitely waterfront. Enough left over for another piece of prime real estate? Check out those ranches and farms—girlhood pony fantasies can really go wild there. There are just so many options to choose from, and located all over the world. Where does all this money come from, anyway? Who knows? But when you are reincarnated as immorally, hyperbolically super-rich, you're going to know how to live in style and where to spend your loot.

44

THE ULTIMATE

Laugh

When you need to press the mommy pause button, go to a kid-free zone, log on to YouTube.com, and search for these videos. There's nothing like watching a cat eating spaghetti to help you forget your troubles. We dare you not to laugh.

Girl licks pickle

Fat cat watches TV

Baby Charlie bit me

Panda sneezes

Cat eats spaghetti

Wedding first dance

Will Ferrell the Landlord

Matt Damon Jimmy Kimmel

Ben Affleck Jimmy Kimmel

Declare a Woman's Right to Shoes

What is it about shoes? We've always loved them, and as moms, our relationship with them has only gotten stronger. Perhaps it's because no matter how much baby weight we've gained, the shoe always fits.

Give yourself permission to jump on the sole train. Browse for them. Fondle them. Buy them. Then, wear a particularly divine pair of strappy sandals next time you make a school lunch or change a dirty diaper.

Snoopy Come Home

Here's how to be a busybody without embarrassment: Log onto overheardinnewyork.com, the website that compiles snippets of real conversations about sex, fashion, relationships, you name it. It's a great way to get out of your own world for a few minutes and snoop with abandon.

PREGNANT WOMAN ON CELL: "So, yeah, I'm about five centimeters dilated, so I'm going to get a Tasti D-Lite and then go to the hospital."

FORTY-SOMETHING WOMAN: "And then I realized that my biggest problem in life is that most of the time I'm incredibly happy, but I'm not aware of how happy I am."

FIFTY-SOMETHING WOMAN: "When she was a newborn, she looked exactly like Yoda, and then she grew up into Dopey."

LITTLE GIRL: "Mommy, Mommy, look! That doggie is pee-peeing on the sidewalk!"
MOM: "Yeah, just like Daddy did last night."

Park It

Arrive early to pick up your child at school, and watch the other mothers passive-aggressively vie for the good spots in the car-pool lane. It's a relatively new sport—as competitive as NASCAR—and just as entertaining.

THE ULTIMATE

Chocolate Indulgence

Ah, chocolate. It's the one thing other than your child's smile that's guaranteed to make you melt. If you're ready to live la vida cocoa, find a way to get your hands on some really fine chocolate (screw the Hershey's Miniatures). Think of these indulgences as Tiffany jewels, precious morsels to savor. The best time of day to eat chocolate is actually in the morning (really!), when your palate is clean and at its peak. Then, follow these simple guidelines from the Manhattan-based chocolate-maker Maribel Lieberman, the owner of MarieBelle New York:

APPEARANCE

Fine chocolate is really an edible work of art. Pay close attention to the deep color and shape. Experiment with a piece of chocolate that resembles a beautiful mosaic or a tiny present. Pretty packaging elevates the experience, as does a gorgeous little plate or a cloth napkin.

TASTE AND TEXTURE

Notice the sensation when the chocolate touches your tongue. Is it velvety smooth, or does it have an unexpected crunch? Close your eyes, and savor the taste. A nibble of a white chocolate bar might reveal an infusion of fresh fruit essence. Does it take a moment for you to pick up on the smoky pistachios hiding inside? Wait a minute, you've just gotten a hit of sweet fig and walnuts. Oh, my, my, my, this is getting good!

PAIRINGS

To build on the experience, enjoy your chocolate with a cup of tea or a glass of wine or champagne. Or try a liquid chocolate experience:

MARIEBELLE ICED CHOCOLATE WITH ORANGE JUICE

½ cup orange juice
½ cup MarieBelle Aztec Iced Chocolate powder
2 cups ice

In a saucepan over medium heat, bring the orange juice to a boil, and then remove from heat. Add the chocolate powder immediately, and mix until well melted. In a blender, add the ice and the chocolate-and-OJ mixture, and blend until you achieve a smooth, icy consistency. Enjoy at once!

Find Love in the Afternoon

CONTRIBUTOR:
Laurie Gelman
mother of two and TV personality

LAURIE'S TIP

Just before I pick up my girls from school, I fill a cup with steaming hot water, take two chunks of dark chocolate from the freezer, go sit on my bed, and watch ten minutes of whatever romantic DVD happens to be in my machine. It's usually one of the many versions of *Pride and Prejudice* or something with Tom Hanks and Meg Ryan. It is truly ten minutes that replenish my soul.

Feel Whole Again

Visit a gorgeous gourmet market such as Whole Foods. Just passing through the electronic doors will transport you to another place. You are Dorothy, over the natural-foods rainbow, and this is your Oz, where everything is in Technicolor, shiny, delicious—and prepared by somebody else.

For ten minutes, you are pampered. (Care for warm miso dressing and wilted greens to complement your seared sesame beef? Yes, please!)

You are smarter. (Thirty-six different kinds of mushrooms? Do tell!)

And ultimately, you are guilt-free. After all, why cook dinner for the kids when you can pick up Organic Citrus-Kissed Chicken Fingers with a side of root-vegetable fries?

THE ULTIMATE

Retail Therapy

New Cyndi tote from Chloé: $2,200. Wooden sailboat puzzle for your son: $30. Ten uninterrupted minutes to shop online? Priceless . . .

There's no time to waste! Get your bookmarks ready. If we could give awards to the sites that have really helped us out in a pinch, they would be:

Best Place to Get Diapers, Dog Toys, DVDs,
and a De'Longhi Toaster in One Click:
AMAZON.COM

Most Transporting Experience If You
Can't Actually Travel to Belize:
ANTHROPOLOGIE.COM

Most Design-Savvy Clothing and
Furniture for the Under-Six Set:
ENFANTTERRIBLESHOP.COM

Best Guilty Pleasure Minus the Guilt:
BAGBORROWORSTEAL.COM

Most Unique Gift Site for All Things Handmade:
ETSY.COM

Most Wallet-Friendly Designer Clothing and Accessories:
BLUEFLY.COM

Best Porn Alternative for Moms:
CONTAINERSTORE.COM

Quickest Way to Feel Like a Kid Again:
DYLANSCANDYBAR.COM

Favorite Way for Fashionistas to Blow a Paycheck:
NETAPORTER.COM

Most Adored Children's Boutique for the Chic:
RONROBINSONINC.COM/LIFESIZEKIDS

52

★★★★★

Neaten Your Nest

CONTRIBUTOR:
Cynthia Rowley
mother of two and clothing designer

CYNTHIA'S TIP

There's so much disorganization in our house, every time I find myself with a few spare minutes, I pick an area and try to make a dent. Someday my spice rack will be alphabetized and my dinner napkins will be perfectly pressed, starched, and color-coded—but until then, I'm psyched to get through the magazine rack and everything with freezer burn. If I just had a free week or two, I'm sure I could make some headway in my closet.

Become the Kid Again

TOOLS NEEDED:
Telephone with a number that cannot be traced

HI, IS HUGH JASS THERE?

When you just can't stomach hearing yourself use the Mommy Voice for one more minute, make a prank phone call.

WHO'S CALLING? OLIVER. OLIVER CLOTHESOFF.

Or watch an elaborate one on YouTube. And if you're feeling really naughty, prank *your* mother.

TELL THEM I. P. FREELY SENT YA.

Get Your Kicks

TOOLS NEEDED:
Soccer ball, cool beverage

While playing soccer with your child, kick the ball deep into the woods, then race over to a lawn chair and sip a tall glass of iced tea until he or she returns. Instant quiet time!

Snack Well

Here's a fast and easy recipe to enjoy with your martini that is also healthy, low-cal, and just as delish as the real thing.

NATURAL NACHOS

- 1 whole-grain flour tortilla
  Vegetable-oil spray
  Sea salt, to taste
- ¼ avocado, mashed
- ¼ tomato, chopped
  Juice from ¼ lemon
  Pepper, to taste

Place the tortilla on a cookie sheet, and lightly coat both sides with vegetable spray (Spectrum makes a great one, but any brand will do). Sprinkle with sea salt. Slice into eighths (make eight wedges). Bake at 350° F for ten minutes.

Place the avocado and tomato in a small bowl, and pour in the lemon juice. Add salt and pepper to taste. Top the baked tortilla with the avocado-tomato mixture and enjoy!

This snack is high in fiber, high in healthy monounsaturated fats (good for your skin!), under 175 calories, and simply delicious.

CONTRIBUTOR: KERI GLASSMAN, MOTHER OF TWO AND AUTHOR OF *THE SNACK FACTOR DIET*

56

*****

Take a Bath With a View

CONTRIBUTOR:
Catherine Malandrino
mother of one and clothing designer

CATHERINE'S TIP

I have always surrounded myself with friends who nourish my spirit and my creativity, and getting together to share a few glasses of pastis at a favorite café is a wonderful way to relax. But when I have time at home, I take a Japanese bath with Shiseido products. My bathroom in New York has an incredible view of the Hudson River, and for me, watching the river is like taking a walk in front of the Seine! Listening to Mary J. Blige makes the experience very relaxing. When it's time to get dressed, I never forget a few drops of jasmine on my neck, and to add a cuff and an oversized ring to my outfit. It's important that a woman wears clothes that are irresistible, and that she feels desirable when she gets dressed!

Book It

If you miss the days when you actually had the time or the energy to read something longer than *Goodnight Moon*, don't despair. There are ways to keep your reading list current without involving actual *books*.

Get a book on CD, or download a great podcast and take the story with you. For a fee, Audible.com offers thousands of book titles, or check out NPR.org for free podcasts. If you're interested in business, summary.com offers a genius service that condenses the top business books each year into succinct eight-page texts and twenty-minute audio summaries (kind of like CliffsNotes for moms). Then, the next time you're in the car, on the treadmill, at the DMV, or the A&P, bring your MP3 player and turn even the most mundane task into a great mini escape.

Take a Mind Trip

Plan your next vacation. Start by fantasizing about your perfect locale, be it Fiji or Paris or the Galápagos Islands. Imagine yourself stepping off the plane and walking into your ideal accommodations. Luxury hotel or rustic hut? Simple backpack or Louis Vuitton steamer? Imagine what you'll eat, what you'll drink, and what you'll see. Then, scour the Internet, travel books, newspapers, and magazines to fill in tangible details.

Give yourself time to dream, too. About the waiter who has just brought you frozen grapes and an iced washcloth. Or the massage being arranged for you by your attentive, loving, appreciative, hardworking, sex-crazed travel companion (also known as your husband). What's that? Oh, your child is

tapping at the bedroom door. "Mommy, you were dreaming."

COME BACK FROM YOUR MOM-CATION . . .

Gloss Over It

TOOL NEEDED:
Department store

When you look good, you feel good. Or so the saying goes. But if your time-starved makeup routine has been whittled down to concealer and ChapStick (on a good day), why not put yourself in the hands of the good people at the department-store makeup counter? A free makeover might be just what the mommy ordered.

The upside: generous samples, abundant compliments, and the amusing questions they'll ask without any trace of irony, like "What is your system?" (*Democratic?*) or "Are you interested in looking ten years younger?" (*Nah!*)

The downside: You could end up looking more like a drag queen than a diva. (It's wise not to do this immediately before an important appointment.) But chances are you'll walk away feeling polished and pampered.

Make That Change

Go through your husband's and children's pants pockets. Start a slush fund by keeping any loose change you find. After all, finders keepers!

Admit They're Really Not Just Like Us

TOOL NEEDED:
$4 to buy *Us Weekly*

Ah, the power of a cool beverage, a comfy place to lounge, and ten minutes with a trashy celebrity magazine. So many moms told us their secret escape involves *Us Weekly* that we'd be remiss in not devoting at least one page to it. Admittedly, it is pure mind drivel, but for $3.99 a pop, we say, go ahead! Don't be ashamed. As vices go, things could be much, much worse.

It's especially amusing to read the in-depth coverage of celebrity moms. You know the ones who—one week after giving birth—are so in love with their babies, have lost all of their pregnancy weight, and are still "managing" a date night with their hubbies. (They never seem to mention that they employ three nannies, live with their personal trainer, and just sold the baby pictures for $3 million.) Before you get too carried away pining over Suri's latest Burberry smock, remember: They've got the annual "Stars Without Makeup" issue to contend with.

Soak Up the Sun

TOOLS NEEDED:
Sunscreen, a squishy chair, a patch of lawn—or better yet,
a hammock

When it's too early in the day for a Mommy Martini, reclaim your sunny disposition by finding a solo spot in the sun. Lather on the sunscreen, close your eyes, feel the warmth on your skin, and let the serotonin work its magic—you'll feel better in minutes. Pretend your sunny patch has a force field around it that makes your ears immune to the word "Mommmmmmm." If your kids question this, explain that you get special powers from the sun—it's how superheroes recharge.

Keep Up with the Kids

If you're tired of not understanding a word your tweens are saying—or rather, *texting*—(WTF?) go to your bedroom, lock the door and let your fingers do the walking. No, we're not talking about *that* (though that is a good idea too, LOL). Take out the BlackBerry and practice your IM terms. You'd be surprised how EZ it is. Now, we're NGL (not gonna lie), texting is not as intuitive as it was back in the day when you wrote "2Good2B4Gotten" in your junior-high yearbook, KWIM (know what I mean)? (Case in point: MTE is "My Thoughts Exactly" not "Mom Takes Ecstasy.") But TTLY (totally) don't let that stop you. Hell, even Winnie the Pooh's friend Tigger says "TTFN"—that's "Ta Ta for Now," for you moms with ADD. Just think, you'll never have to ask your kids WDYMBT (What Do You Mean By That) again. G2G!

HERE ARE SOME HELPFUL TERMS TO GET YOU STARTED:

LOL—LAUGHING OUT LOUD
LMAO—LAUGHING MY ASS OFF
IDK—I DON'T KNOW
BRB—BE RIGHT BACK
TTYL—TALK TO YOU LATER
POS—PARENT OVER SHOULDER
KPC—KEEPING PARENTS CLUELESS
IMHO—IN MY HUMBLE OPINION
LYLAS—LOVE YOU LIKE A SISTER
ZZZ—SLEEPING, BORED, TIRED
G2G—GOT TO GO

THE ULTIMATE

Nap

Preschoolers love them. College kids can't live without them. Even Napoleon, JFK, and Margaret Thatcher were big fans of naps.

Burrowing under a light blanket of sleep in the middle of a busy day is not unlike digging an escape tunnel, one that bypasses crazy kids, impossible work situations, and your non-stop Mommy life. So give yourself permission to play hide-and-sleep. And remember, you're not being lazy—it's Mommy survival. You'll emerge with more patience, productivity, and an improved mom-itude.

Here are some suggestions for a yummy ten-minute snooze:

- Find a clean, quiet place, free of distractions. (We know, we know. Just do your best with this one!)
- The ideal times to nap are in the morning or just after lunch, if possible.
- Slip into something more comfortable, like a pair of your hubby's cotton boxers, a silk nightgown, or a big old college T-shirt.
- Try to avoid consuming food or beverages containing caffeine, fat, or sugar before you nap. They hinder your ability to sleep.

- Darken your nap area by drawing the blinds. While you're at it, why not wear one of those fabulous little satin eyeshades like Lucille Ball used to wear in *I Love Lucy*?

- Raise the room temperature slightly, or use a blanket to keep you toasty. Egyptian cotton bedding or Frette sheets and a cashmere throw will make the nap even more delicious.

- Light a scented candle to give the room a peaceful glow. We like the Seda France Classic Toile Candle in Japanese Quince.

- Don't forget to set your alarm clock to wake yourself up. Try waking to a calming sound such as classical music.

Take a Zen Ten

A quick meditation session can cause a stressed-out brain to do a U-turn. Next time you feel the onset of a Mommy meltdown, take these steps. You'll feel the benefits inside and out.

1. Sit up tall at the edge of a chair, and situate your feet hip-width apart.
2. Place your hands on your thighs, palms facing down, and close your eyes.
3. Inhale and exhale deeply while mentally repeating the mantra, "Breathing in, I calm my body. Breathing out, I smile." Allow yourself to smile if it feels natural.
4. After about six minutes, let go of the mantras and observe your breath for a minute until you bring yourself back to reality.

Use Your Words

TOOLS NEEDED:
pen and paper, pretty journal or stationery

Freestyle writing is a great way to clear your head. Sit with a pad and pen, and write down whatever comes to mind. Ignore grammar or any such rules, and write about anything—love, politics, puppies. It's amazing how simply putting words on paper can help clarify your thoughts.

Or try keeping a laid-back version of a journal. Forget pondering the meaning of life (who's got the time?) and instead write a sentence or two about get-togethers, appointments, even errands. It's amazingly fun to go back to past entries and marvel at the everyday details you would have otherwise forgotten, like the sweater your son insisted on wearing eight days in a row, or the adorable thing your daughter said in the bathtub. For the digital-minded mom, check out software such as LifeJournal (for Windows) or MacJournal (for the Mac), which enables you to add photos and video clips to your entries, as well as text.

(Re)Order in the House

TOOLS NEEDED:
Trash bags, paint, elbow grease

When you need a big time-out, like when all the vodka in Russia won't help, try rearranging your house. Paint walls. Move furniture. Fill bags for the Salvation Army truck. Often, when

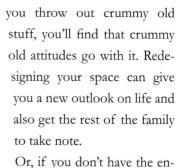

you throw out crummy old stuff, you'll find that crummy old attitudes go with it. Redesigning your space can give you a new outlook on life and also get the rest of the family to take note.

Or, if you don't have the energy to actually move (let alone move furniture), why not watch someone else do it? TiVo a makeover show on HGTV. Watch the Before and After at real-time speed, and zip through the middle. It's the next best thing to doing it yourself, and you can experience an entire transformation in ten minutes flat.

Give Hef the Heave-Ho

Write a fantasy letter to Hugh Heffner, explaining how you're flattered but need to decline being featured in the next *Playboy* MILF edition.

69
★★★★★

THE ULTIMATE

Solo-Sex Break

CONTRIBUTOR:
Dr. Logan Levkoff
mother of one, sexologist, author of *Third Base Ain't What It Used to Be: What Your Kids Are Learning About Sex Today— and How to Teach Them to Become Sexually Healthy Adults*

LOGAN'S TIP

Some people think that women need a lot more than ten minutes to have a fabulous sexual experience. With a partner, that's true. More often than not we need foreplay; we crave it. However, when we are alone, sometimes ten minutes is all it takes for us to have a fulfilling experience. We know what it takes for us to be sufficiently aroused.

The ultimate sexual time-out is about setting the mood and turning on. Put on your favorite music, read passages from your favorite erotica, or flip on some pornography. Get comfortable, relax, and spend some quality time with your favorite vibrating accessory. Having an orgasm does wonders for recharging our sex drives and our overall health. So the more we have, the better off we (and our partners) are. And don't forget, you can plan for these moments in advance. Visit your favorite erotic boutique (a personal favorite is Kiki De Monteparnasse—and yes, they have a website, too!) and shop for some good erotic material such as books or films. Preparing in advance can prolong the turn-on; you will be waiting with anticipation for your ten minutes alone!

And a word to the wise: Make sure you always have some extra AA batteries handy. There is nothing worse than a vibrator that dies in the heat of the moment!

Try a Hair Blowout for Cheaters

TOOLS NEEDED:
Hair dryer, round brush, hair rollers, hair spray, mousse, and hair glaze

Getting your hair blown out at the salon is a surefire way for mom to feel like a million bucks. But unless you're Mia Farrow circa 1970, ten minutes just won't suffice. So here's a shortcut method that can work in a pinch: Section off the hair that begins at your outer eyebrows and reaches your crown. This will form two small triangles of hair on each side of your head. Blow out smooth. Then, work mousse through the rest of the hair underneath it, and let it air-dry. The idea is for the top half of your hair to look smooth and cover the rest. Shhhhhh—we won't tell.

Another secret weapon? Hair rollers. Yes, the kind that Grandma used to use. Only these are the kind you plug in. Conair's ionic rollers heat up in two minutes flat and require only three minutes on your head to create soft ringlets. Spritz on a little hair spray—and voilà! Instant polish.

If your hair is looking dull and tired, amp up the luster with a quick at-home hair glaze (we like Frédéric Fekkai Salon Glaze). For the best results, wash your hair with a clarifying shampoo first so it will be primed to soak up the silicone-based treatment. Then apply the glaze, let it penetrate into your strands, and rinse. Your hair will be red carpet–worthy.

Get High on Fidelity

TOOLS NEEDED:
Wedding album and/or video

Holy Matrimony! Is that really *you* in that white dress? Pop in your wedding video, or dust off your wedding album and remind yourself of the romantic time when it was just you and your husband. Remember the way you looked at each other. Relive your first dance. Ask yourself what on earth you were thinking when you chose those chartreuse bridesmaids' dresses. And dream about the days when you could see a movie on a whim, sleep till noon, and have sex any time you wanted. Sigh. Sure, he had more hair, and you were a size smaller back then. But really, don't you agree that life has only gotten sweeter now that you've got a family? (Here's the part where you say, "I do!")

Break Free

TOOL NEEDED:
BlackBerry or computer

While sitting on the train or waiting in the car-pool lane, there is no better way to escape the everyday madness than to play a game or two of BrickBreaker. If you're a BrickBreaker virgin, we're talking about the very basic game that comes with the BlackBerry, but you can also play it online. You've got a paddle at the bottom. You launch a ball up into the air to hit bricks. You try to make all of the bricks go away. (Break, break, break, bomb.)

Moms everywhere have admitted they have a BrickBreaker "problem." Why? Maybe it's the mindless simplicity (break, break, break, catch), the portability (break, break, break, shoot), the repetition (break, break, break, flip), or the feeling of actually accomplishing something by clearing a row of bricks. (Drat! Lost another life.)

Chat rooms reveal players so addicted to the game that they admit to neglecting their jobs or literally dreaming about the game.

Hello, my name is Mom and I'm a BrickBreaker addict . . .

Sneak In a Sit-Up

Finding sixty minutes to work out can seem downright impossible when you can't get sixty seconds to pee. So try to find opportunities for exercise that are already hiding themselves in your daily routine.

Pushing the stroller at a fast speed, doing calf stretches on the checkout line, even vacuuming can give you the chance to work up a good sweat, if you do it purposefully. Park the car at the far end of the lot so you'll need to walk farther to your destination. Take the stairs instead of the elevator. Or sneak in exercise in nontraditional places. We know one mom who does arm circles in the private bathroom at work. Hey, if your coworkers can go outside and smoke five times a day, why not?

74

★★★★★

Drive, She Said

CONTRIBUTOR:

Lara Spencer

mother of two and TV personality

LARA'S TIP

I love taking the long way home from the studio when we are done for the day. Putting the top down on my convertible, feeling the late-afternoon sun on my skin, listening to Coldplay or John Mayer as I cruise along Mulholland Drive. The view of the valley and the hills are so beautiful. It only adds ten minutes to the trip, but it feels like I am a world away.

Power Down

TOOLS NEEDED:
Peaceful place to hide (a walk-in closet works nicely)

When your life is beginning to resemble a Calgon commercial—sans bubble bath—hit the mommy pause button and turn off all of your electronic devices: PDA, cell phone, computer. For ten whole minutes, go somewhere quiet and remain unplugged. If someone important questions why you were not reachable, tell him or her that your child flushed your BlackBerry down the toilet.

★★★★★

Join the Crew

CONTRIBUTOR:
Jill Kargman
mother of three and author of *Momzillas*

JILL'S TIP

My love affair with the J.Crew catalog began in boarding school, back in ye olde days before the Internet link to the outside. As my dorm lacked the levels of intrigue of, say, Hogwarts, I was elated when the new J.Crew arrived in my mailbox. The colors were an escape unto themselves—brown was never brown, it was hedgehog. Gray was smokestack, pink was passionfruit, red was firebird. Now, it's better than ever. When I get in bed with a thick novel, it can be too dense. With a celeb tabloid mag, I feel too shallow. J.Crew is just right for that dreamy, ten-minute, breezy jaunt to Marrakech or Maine, savoring bright blues and greens, spices and sand. As a mom of three kids under six, we don't get to travel much anymore. So it's kind of like I'm back in school, dreaming of beaches and Parisian streets. So thanks, J.Crew, for transporting me once again for a ten-minute journey through crisp, chic, clean style where I can turn off my brain and just browse not merely item numbers, but a metallic flip-flop lifestyle. I don't know what that "J" stands for, but for me there will always be something about it that is very, very Jill.

Become a Woman of Letters

TOOLS NEEDED:
Pen, stationery, stamps

In an age when even birth announcements are sent by e-mail (and let's be honest, quickly deleted), why not go old-school and write a real letter? From love letters to apology letters, thank-you letters to erotic letters, the personal note is a lost art and something to savor.

Make the experience extra special by using a beautiful pen and gorgeous stationery. Play a great piece of music to get you in the mood. Enclose a treasure such as a pressed flower or a recent photo of the kids. Or have your little one doodle on the outside of the envelope with bright crayons before you mail it. Then, imagine the recipient spotting your colorful note among the bills and the junk mail. Who knows, your masterpiece just might inspire him or her to write one back.

Lather on La Mer

Pampered women around the globe know that La Mer is the greatest moisturizing cream on the market. But at $150 an ounce, we're thinking you might not want to blow your child's college tuition on a case of it. So for those everyday moments when your skin needs a quick pick-me-up, try substituting Burt's Bees Baby Bee Apricot Baby Oil instead. Your body will feel smooth, nourished, and as soft as your baby's tush (and you'll still be able to afford Harvard).

Get a Bloom for Your Room

TOOLS NEEDED:
Florist, less than $10

Lilacs and freesia and peonies, oh my! When you need to remind yourself that there's an actual woman inside the mom,
say it with flowers. Visit an expensive florist in your neighborhood once a week, and have your child pick out a single, delicious stem for your bedside table. It's a little thing that will fill
your bedroom with a gorgeous fragrance and make you feel
special all week long.

THE ULTIMATE

Bath

It's almost a cliché, the image of Mom luxuriating in the perfect claw-foot tub, basking in the soft glow of 100 votive candles strategically placed around her spotless bathroom.

Sound familiar? We thought not. Because if you're anything like us, your bathroom is probably smallish, cluttered with kids' bath toys, and sorely lacking in the serenity department. So here's a way to transform your bath experience in ten minutes or less that does not require you to scrape melted wax out of 100 votive candles when you're through. It's called JellyBath (jellybath.com). Developed in Japan (where they've got this bathing thing mastered) and used in spas worldwide, a JellyBath is a warm, thick, creamy gel infused with aromatherapy oils. Add it to warm water and it turns into a fluffy, translucent "jelly" that smells delicious, soothes aching muscles, and enables you to soak away the cares of the day. Thousands of tiny beads contained in the gel create a "bath blanket" that retains heat up to four times longer than a normal bath. We like it because it's fast, easy, inexpensive, and all-natural. Perfect for a maxed-out mom on a mission.

Click and Brag

Do grown-up women still play with dolls? See for yourself at dressupchallenge.com. Sign up, and you'll get a new challenge to dress up your avatar (that's "online doll" to you) while competing against other players. The fun part is the community: You can look at one another's creations, give awards, boast about your doll, and—if you so choose—even chat about your *real* life.

If dolls aren't your thing, here are some other addictive online games to try:

- dinerdash.com
- bejeweled.com
- facade.com/iching (where you can do an online *IChing* reading and see what the future holds)

Make Like a Tree

CONTRIBUTOR:
Gabby Karan DeFelice
mother of three, designer, and entrepreneur

GABBY'S TIP

The best Mommy time I take is to practice my yoga. If I am able to carve two hours out of my day, I go to the Jivamukti Yoga Center in New York City. And when I really need a long time-out, I go to our place on Parrot Kay, for a yoga retreat with Rodney Yee. But if you've only got ten minutes, Tree Pose is really helpful for centering yourself and practicing balance in your life. Here's how to do Tree Pose.

1. Begin by standing up straight with both arms at your sides.
2. Inhale, and shift the bulk of your weight onto your left foot. Exhale, and bend your right knee, placing the sole of your right foot as high as possible onto your left inner thigh.
3. Point your toes down, steady yourself, and take a deep breath.
4. Next, raise your arms to shoulder level, and stretch them out from the middle of your back. Lift your chest, and look straight ahead.
5. Now, bring your palms together as if you are saying a prayer. Inhale as you raise your arms overhead, keeping your palms together and stretching upward through your fingertips.
6. Repeat on the other leg.

Come out of the Closet

When your schedule allows for very little time in boutiques, "shop" your closet instead. Try on all the wonderful outfits you rarely get to wear anymore: fancy dresses, sexy heels, sequins—go wild! Then, take a glass of champagne onto your balcony (or onto your back porch, if you have a house), and enjoy feeling fabulous—until the next poopie Pull Up appears.

Have Fun at Their Expense

TOOLS NEEDED:
a food processor, vegetables

You love motherhood, but sometimes you just need to let your Evil Mommy flag fly. When those moments hit, sneak pureed cauliflower into their mac and cheese. They'll never detect it. Then feel smug and self-satisfied knowing that they're unwittingly scarfing down a daily serving of veggies.

Find Your "Be" Time

CONTRIBUTOR:
Keisha Whitaker
mother of three and television personality

KEISHA'S TIP

I try to take minibreaks from house, hubby, and girls *often*. It's a must! I will sneak in a day movie—usually a comedy or a chick flick—when the girls are at camp or school. Or I may get a manicure and pedicure and catch up on my mags.

One of my favorite time-outs is to wake up a li'l early—maybe just a few minutes before *everyone* else—and just sit and breathe. I take inventory of my life and all its blessings, things I want to accomplish, and things I want to change. It's great because the house is quiet, and I can hear the sounds from outside. I take it all in. It's so serene and peaceful—my time to just *be*.

See the Light

Looking for a great cure for pale, tired skin? Drop into a salon and try LED light therapy. It takes only a few minutes, and you'll love the results.

LED light therapy is a noninvasive procedure done with panels of red and/or infrared lights that work to activate skin cells. Sort of like photosynthesis for the skin, it utilizes light energy already found in skin cells to promote healing and antiaging effects.

Effective on stretch marks, cellulite, acne, and skin pigmentation, it also works to reduce scarring (great for after a C-section). Most important, this therapy also increases endorphins, so you not only look great, you also feel fabulous as a result!

CONTRIBUTOR: ILDI PEKAR, MOTHER OF ONE AND OWNER OF THE ILDI PEKAR SKIN CARE SALON IN NEW YORK CITY.

Whip It Good

The contents of your fridge can help you *feel* delicious too. Try this recipe for an energizing green smoothie and give the Energizer Bunny a run for his money.

Fill a blender three quarters full with a combination of organic spinach, lettuce, and parsley. Then, fill the last quarter of the blender with the following suggested ingredients:

1 cup juice or water
  Banana
1 cup frozen organic berries
2 tablespoons ground flax seeds
  Cucumber
1 fresh-squeezed lemon

The above ingredients are optional, and you can add or remove them according to your taste. The more green stuff, the better!

Sit in Judgment

If arguments with your spouse about parenting issues have ever made you wonder, "What in the world was I thinking when I married this man?" log on to weddingbetting.com and take out your angst on total strangers.

A picture of newlyweds will prompt you to answer the question *How long will this couple last?* With nothing more than a brief description to go on, you vote: Happily Ever After, 15 years, 8 years, 5 years, 1 year, or Barely Past the Altar.

What makes this addictive is the way the site constantly presents new couples, prompting you to vote again and again and again—until you finally turn off your computer and realize you've forgotten why you were annoyed with your husband in the first place.

Return to Fantasy Island

TOOLS NEEDED:
Computer, a fruity cocktail, appropriate background music. (Come on, fully embrace this exercise! Download "Kokomo" by the Beach Boys.)

Set up a photo slide show on your computer of a fabulous vacation you took in your pre-mommy life. As you press play, sit back, relax, and remember when trips did not include Kids Clubs, chicken nuggets, or your mom flap.

90

★★★★★

THE ULTIMATE

"Power Ten" Workout

CONTRIBUTOR:
Jennifer Maanavi
mother of two and owner of New York fitness studio
Physique 57

JENNIFER'S TIP

If the last time you used your gym membership card was to unlock your front door (forgot the keys again—baby brain strikes again!) you know how hard it is to get back into shape. Who has the time, energy, and motivation to make it to an aerobics class when you're on the two a.m. feeding shift? Well, no need for a fancy gym when you've got these exercises which come from a technique devised by Lotte Berk, a famous British ballerina. Here are some basics you can do anywhere (no bar required). You'll be fitting back into those Current/Elliott jeans in no time. Ready, set, go!

TRICEPS

Facing away from a chair, place your hands behind you on its seat, fingers facing forward and arms straight. Put your legs out straight in front of you. Lower yourself a few inches by bending your arms. Then, return to the starting position. You might need to bend your legs, but keep them as straight as possible for a stronger workout. Do two sets of 20.

ABS

Lie on the floor with a pillow under your lower back, and straighten your legs holding a playground ball between your feet. Roll the ball toward your seat, with the ball remaining between your feet. Then straighten your legs again. Do two sets of 20.

THIGHS

Start on your knees, and sit back on your heels. Stretch your arms overhead. Using your thigh muscles, lift your seat off your heels. Then, lower back down. Repeat 20 times. For a more intense burn, try lifting your seat and moving your hips from side to side for a few counts. Then, lower to your heels.

Get Your Fix

CONTRIBUTOR:
Abby Pecoriello

mother of two and author of *Crafty Mama: Makes 49 Fast, Fabulous, Foolproof (Baby & Toddler) Projects*

ABBY'S TIP

There's nothing more therapeutic to me than fixing something. I'm not talking about washing machines or car transmissions. I'm referring to the simple stuff that I know I can make better in about seven minutes. I hot-glue a tiara back together, re-bead a necklace that my daughter broke, or mend a book that my little one ate. Or if there's nothing that's actually physically broken, I "fix" things by making them jazzier! I'll add rhinestones to $8 Vans sneaks from Wal-Mart, or iron a funny picture of Urkel onto my daughter's plain ol' T-shirt.

When I'm in my time-out-meditative-super-fix-it-mama mode, I don't listen to music or TV or multitask by talking on the phone. That wouldn't be relaxing at *all*. I like to focus on the simple task at hand and ultimately achieve an easy success. I'm always thinking so much about everything—my kids, my fam, money, work, school. This is the one time that all I need to worry about is whether the tiara is durable enough to withstand seventeen more dress-up sessions.

Gossip, Girl

Go through the Missed Calls log on your cell phone for the past month, and make note of the friends you need to call back. Then, next time you have a moment (like when your child is happily tapping the keyboard of a Mac at the Apple Store), you'll know who to dial first. As corny as it may sound, there's nothing like a grown-up gab with a girlfriend to perk things up. Think of it as Mommy Recess.

Get Lucky

TOOLS NEEDED:
$1, a lottery ticket

Sometimes all it takes to feel like you've hit the jackpot is to look into your child's angelic face. But for those moments when the only thing that will cheer you up is cold hard cash, enter the lottery. That's right, buy a good old-fashioned lottery ticket, and fantasize about the first five things you'd do with $50 million.

Maybe it's buying that million-dollar beach house or dropping $25,000 at Christian Louboutin without a second thought. Perhaps it's taking your mom-tourage on a five-star spa vacation. Then again, employing a personal chef, a trainer and a live-in housekeeper sounds mighty good.

Of course, it's not really about winning. But there now, didn't we get your mind off your troubles for a few minutes?

Admire Kelly's Grace

CONTRIBUTOR:
Wen Zhou
mother of two, CEO, and President of Phillip Lim

WEN'S TIP

I love Kelly Hoppen's books. I am redesigning my town house, and her gorgeous design books are a great inspiration for ideas. Hoppen is an avatar of the hip, high-end interior design that is celebrated in the pages of *Architectural Digest*, *In Style*, and the *New York Times*. Her cool, modernist aesthetic is at once timeless and at the cutting edge of style today. Her book *Kelly Hoppen Home* offers readers a chance to learn from her chic design philosophy. Giving a clear picture of her approach at every stage—from the conception of an idea, through preparation and decision making, to implementing plans and achieving a reality—Hoppen shares her insider secrets and reveals how to get the most from a living space.

Hire a Granny

Sometimes Mommy just needs to be babied. When those moments arise, log on to netgranny.ch, an inspired website that invites you into the living rooms of real-life Swiss grandmothers who will knit you a pair of socks. (No kidding!) Just seeing photos of the lovely, silver-haired nanas is oddly comforting. Select your favorite by clicking on your desired grandma's photo and placing your order. In a few weeks, your package will arrive. If only she could deliver it in person, along with a warm batch of oatmeal cookies . . .

Now, About Those Cookies...

It really *is* possible to get a plate of warm cookies delivered to your door in the middle of the night. Just call Insomnia Cookies (insomniacookies.com), the all-natural-cookie delivery service.

Place your order, and about thirty minutes later lucky moms living in certain regions of the United States can feast on the chocolate-chunk-peanut-butter-chip-white-chocolate-macadamia-nut confection of their choice. They'll even bring you a glass of cold milk to wash it down. (For moms in the rest of the country, overnight shipping is available).

Now, can somebody please tuck us in?

Sing . . . Sing a Song!

TOOLS NEEDED:
a stereo, privacy

There's no better way to rock your time-out than to belt out a great tune. Moms everywhere have listed this as their number one foolproof escape in the car, the kitchen, the shower—even the closet. From sound tracks (*Hairspray, Mamma Mia!*) to obscure '80s tunes ("Rock Me Amadeus," Soul II Soul) to TV theme songs (*Family Ties, Golden Girls*), it seems the sound track of your life is as original as you are.

As for us, we're partial to show tunes. So channel your inner Bernadette Peters, and give these great songs a try (hairbrush-microphone optional):

1. "Defying Gravity" from *Wicked* by Stephen Schwartz
2. "Seasons of Love" from *Rent* by Jonathan Larson
3. "Dancing Queen" from *Mamma Mia!* by ABBA
4. "Legally Blonde Remix" from *Legally Blonde* by Laurence O'Keefe and Nell Benjamin
5. "The River Won't Flow" from *Songs for a New World* by Jason Robert Brown

While you're at it, here's a top-five list of great show tunes for your kids to sing too:

1. "Tomorrow" from *Annie* by Charles Strouse and Martin Charnin
2. "Who Better than Me" from *Tarzan* by Phil Collins
3. "Hakuna Matata" from *The Lion King* by Elton John and Tim Rice
4. "We Go Together" from *Grease* by Warren Casey and Jim Jacobs
5. "You Can't Stop the Beat" from *Hairspray* by Marc Shaiman

CONTRIBUTOR: AUDREY KAPLAN, MOTHER OF ONE AND THE FOUNDER OF BROADWAY BABIES/SUPERSTARS/APPLAUSE

98

★★★★★

THE ULTIMATE

No-Pressure Pilates

CONTRIBUTOR:
Erika Bloom
owner of Erika Bloom Pilates Plus in New York City

ERIKA'S TIP

Looking for a great stress-reliever *and* a way to ease posture problems because you're constantly lifting your little ones? Here is a series of ten-minute exercises you can do anywhere. Just prepare a quiet place with a soft rug, exercise mat, or blanket.

BACK BREATHING

Lie on your back with your knees bent and your feet flat on the floor and in line with your hips. Relax your back into the floor, feeling the weight of your hips and the back of your head heavy into the earth. Begin by inhaling and bringing your attention to your breath. Notice how it fills your lungs and expands your rib cage. Staying relaxed, begin to focus the breath into the back of your body so that your rib cage expands back toward the floor. Feel the gentle expansion and then softening of your lower back and your lower-back ribs.
BENEFITS: The movement of the lungs and the diaphragm aid in digestion and help in easing the adrenals, the key organs in stress management.

SUPPORTED GODDESS

Place a couch cushion, a yoga bolster, or a stack of firm blankets on the floor. Sit in front of it with your lower back against the short edge. Bend your knees, place your hands behind your head, and roll back onto the cushion, keeping your pelvis on the floor. Let your knees drop open so the soles of your feet come together and your legs form a diamond shape. Bring your arms out to the sides, palms up, to rest on the floor. Remain in this renewing position for up to five minutes.

BENEFITS: This exercise opens up the muscles of the chest, the arms, the hips, and the abdomen, areas affected by both childbirth and the constant motion of picking up the kids.

SUPPORTED TWIST

Using the same cushion or bolster, turn sideways to place the left side of your hip against the short edge of the cushion, with your legs on the floor comfortably out to your right side, knees bent. Rotate your torso to the left so your hands can touch the floor on either side of the cushion and your chest faces the cushion. Lay your chest and belly down onto the cushion, turning your head to the right, and let your arms widen onto the floor. Relax your entire body into the twist. Breathe deeply into your lungs. Remain in the position for up to three minutes. Repeat on the other side.

BENEFITS: This position lengthens, opens, and relaxes the hips and the entire back. It also helps to wring toxins out of the body.

Go Down Under

TOOLS NEEDED:
Subway fare

The subway is one of the last places on earth where a mom can spend a few minutes without interruption. No phones ringing. No BlackBerries vibrating. No children asking for a snack.

Next time you're on the train, savor the time and collect your thoughts. Daydream about the life of the stranger sitting across from you (Art director? Porn star?). Savor a few minutes of pure pleasure reading. Or just close your eyes and take a few deep breaths before the conductor tells you it's time to get back to life. Stand clear of the closing doors. . . .

Be Good to Yourself

A FEW PARTING WORDS FOR YOU INCREDIBLE MOMS, AMAZING NURTURERS, AND WONDER WOMEN:

Being a mom is important and humbling and amazing. As the m-o-m there will always be those times when you feel like you can't do enough. Or give enough. Or be enough. Overwhelming self-doubt is a prerequisite for the job. That, and the ability to grab things with your feet.

So do yourself a favor and let go of "perfect." Surround yourself with friends who make you feel good. Laugh as much as possible, especially when you are sobbing uncontrollably. Remember the big goal here is to raise healthy, happy, good kids—and enjoy the ride. And finally, don't forget to give YOU permission to take a few minutes to yourself once in a while. Everyone, including your kids, will be glad you did—even if it does take them thirty years to admit it.

xo,

Julie and Lyss

A Special Thanks to Our Amazing Mom Contributors

Words cannot express how grateful we are to all of the moms who shared their incredible time-out ideas. You are a bold, tireless, loving, creative, hilarious, mischievous, and passionate group, and you inspire us to be the best moms that we can be. We only regret that we couldn't put each and every one of your names in bold type on every page of this book.

FOR YOUR MAGIC POWERS AND SUPER STRENGTH, THANK YOU, WONDER WOMEN:

Heba Abedin
June Ambrose
Araks Yeramyan Andrews
Anna Lee Bassani
Lisa Beels
Yvonne Beils
Tanya Zukerbrot Beyer
Tatiana Boncompagni
E.J. Boyce
Allison Brod
Mary-Elizabeth Carrell
Jennifer Cattaui
Gigi Lee Chang
Elizabeth Co
Jess Coffey
Jessica Denay
Kysa Englund
Rachel Felder
Jennifer Feldman
Jennifer Fisher
Margery Frank
Cozy Freedman
Millicent Fortunoff
Michelle Goldman
Marjorie Jaffe Goldner
Kimberly Jason Graham
Stephanie Greenfield
Dena Hammerstein
Annie Hekker

Randi Hirsch
Stephanie Hirsch
Charolette Kashani
Faith Kates
Ruth Katz
Amy Tara Koch
Karen Kreitzer
Thia Longhi
Paulette Stein Meyer
Christine Naylor
Amy Newman
Stephanie Kastor Orenstein
Kimberly Oser
Pam Pariseau
Victoria Pericon
Amanda Poses
Meg Sewell Rosen
Renee Roth
Jan Schillay
Rebecca Sklar Shalam
Heidi Simech
Michelle Smith
Kris Soumas
Karen Ticktin
Dana Wachs
Nancy Weber
Jacqui Weidman
Pamela Weinberg
Kim Weinstein

Acknowledgments

A very special thank-you to our dear friends Amy Jaffe and Keri Levitt for introducing us. You are amazing matchmakers! Without you, this book would have never happened. To our tireless agent at the William Morris Agency, Dorian Karchmar, for championing our book, believing in us, and sharing your own experiences as a super-mom. To our wonderful editor, Judy Pray, and the entire team at Clarkson Potter, for showing tremendous patience with first-time writers. Karen Shapiro, you truly outdid yourself. Thank you for reaching out to so many wonderful and talented mothers and for helping us laugh at 2:00 a.m. To Izak, your gorgeous illustrations just plain make us happy! To our title gods and goddesses: Janine Evangelista, Steve Newman, Tracy Grandstaff, Linda Danner, Marcy Heisler, and Zina Goldrich. To Pam Pariseau, Arky Klappas, Maggie and Dan Scott, Jack, and Carey, for listening, contributing, cheerleading (and babysitting!). To Brian Stern, for working your magic by helping us approach the very best moms to contribute to our book, and for listening to Lyss explain for years that she needs just a few minutes to herself to remain sane and Divalysscious. To John Jamilkowski, for showing your amazing support and never once questioning the wisdom of writing a book three weeks after having a baby. To our delicious children, Jackson, Kate, Oliver, and Tucker, *we love you,* and we are so proud to be your moms 24/7.